THE BATSFORD COLOUR BOOK OF
Dorset

Introduction and commentaries by
John Hyams

B. T. BATSFORD LTD
LONDON & SYDNEY

First published 1975

© John Hyams 1975

Filmset by Servis Filmsetting Ltd, Manchester

Printed by Lee-Fung Asco, Hong Kong
for the publishers B. T. Batsford Ltd, 4 Fitzhardinge Street,
London W1H 0AH and 23 Cross Street, Brookvale, N.S.W.2100, Australia

ISBN 0 7134 3006 0

Contents

Acknowledgments

The Publishers wish to thank the following for permission to reproduce the photographs appearing in this book:

Peter Baker Photography: pages 31 & 33
Noel Habgood FRPS: pages 25, 35 & 61
A F Kersting FRPS: pages 23, 37 & 59
Picturepoint Ltd: pages 41, 49 & 51
Kenneth Scowen FIIP FRPS: pages 19, 21, 27, 29, 43, 47, 53, 55, 57 & 63
Spectrum Colour Library: pages 17, 39 & 45

Introduction

One can summarise the character of some English counties in a phrase, because one's predominant impression of them is formed by an overwhelmingly obvious quality. The South Downs and the contrasting ruin of the coastline signify Sussex, for instance, or featureless flatness, swept and abraded by the easterly winds, Norfolk. Of Dorset, however, everyone has his own image.

For Dorset epitomises all of England except heavy industry, mountains, and moorland. It has chalk downs, heath, green expanses with little undulations and hedgerows; it has woods, coniferous and deciduous; it has old buildings and modern; it has villages still redolent of Hardy's Wessex, and a conurbation parts of which might have been torn out of, say, Watford or bordered the North Circular Road. It has a coast of great variety and often breathtaking beauty, ranging from the gentleness of Poole Harbour to the savage cliffscapes of Purbeck and the variegated majesty of the seaboard west of Bridport.

This diversity raises questions worth answering. Why, for instance, is most of the county agricultural and thinly populated? Why is so much of it by contemporary standards unspoiled? The answer lies in its geology and geography, which together have ensured that neither has heavy industry any reason to come to Dorset, nor even does much traffic between important centres of population pass through it. Into the bargain, it is just too far from London to have suffered the fate of closer areas, which have broken into a plaguey rash of dormitory settlements for commuters.

So Dorset's towns and villages remain on a rather small scale, as they have been through history. Only the large urban area of Poole, together with Bournemouth and Christchurch (which until 1974 were in Hampshire and therefore, speaking historically, do not invalidate this generalisation) is the exception. The county has rarely seen the enactment of any national drama. The murder of King Edward the Martyr at Corfe, the landing of Monmouth at Lyme Regis in 1686, and the condemnation of the Tolpuddle Martyrs in 1834 are its main contributions to the story of England. Otherwise its past is its own, nursed secretively in its valleys and coves and on its remote hilltops.

An understanding of the county must begin with some knowledge of the rocks that shape it. Its core is a great massif of chalk hills which run southwest from Cranborne Chase almost to Beaminster, then turning sharply eastward extend to the coast east of Weymouth. A narrow ridge forms the spine of the Isle of Purbeck, reaching the sea by Swanage.

The northern escarpments of these chalk downs, from Lulworth to Swanage and from Shaftesbury to Bubb Down Hill, offer splendid viewpoints and fine scenery. So sharply do they rear out of the plain below that they produce the illusion of mountains. North Dorset – the Vale of Blackmore with its dairy farms on lush, heavy, clay soil, its villages on narrow strips of limestone, its lanes between wide grass verges and hedgerows – lies below, a panorama of what the English think of as typically English countryside.

The chalk hills themselves are severe and rounded, the flinty soil on their tops often nowadays under the plough, though they were traditionally grazed by sheep. They are fissured by watercourses running in a generally north-south direction, the main roads for the most part leading along them. Consequently travel east and west, which means crossing hills, is possible only by country lane or footpath. Walking in this superb countryside, if farmers have not ploughed out the paths and barricaded them with barbed wire, is, however, very rewarding for the hill tops are unfrequented and the views of distant horizons extensive and plentiful. Northward from, say, High Stoy, Bulbarrow, and Nettlecombe Tout, you can look across mile upon mile of Blackmore Vale, and see to your left and right the precipitous descent into it of the highlands like the gigantically magnified ramparts of one of the prehistoric forts that squat frowningly atop so many of the hills.

The largest of these is Maiden Castle, outside Dorchester. Other examples – and this list is not exhaustive – are Eggardon Hill, Badbury Rings, Hambledon Hill, Hod Hill, Rawlsbury, and Flowers Barrow (on the cliff edge, overlooking Worbarrow Bay). These are all large, dominating their respective summits with a barbarian self-assurance. Sometimes in association with them, sometimes in clusters of their own, groups of barrows lie about the chalk hills, evocative reminders of a remote past whose remains have been obliterated in so much of the rest of Britain.

A barrow, of course, is a tomb, a *memento mori*, and also an affirmation of a spirit world. Two strange monuments to the concern of our pre-Roman forbears with the supernatural contribute to the air of mysteriousness which the Dorset chalklands breathe. The more puzzling archaeologically is the six-mile long cursus, probably a processional way with a religious function, which is traceable, and in part visible, from Thickthorn Down, near Gussage St Michael, as far as the late Roman rampart of Bokerly Dyke, near Pentridge. The other is at Knowlton, not far from Wimborne St Giles. Here, an ancient sacred site surrounded with barrows enwraps the ruins of a twelfth-century church which was set plumb in the middle of a Bronze Age henge, attesting to the continuity through four millennia of some form of worship in this one place.

Only one river actually cuts through the chalk, and that is the Stour. It rises at Stourhead, just north of the border in Wiltshire, and after meandering south through the plain, pierces the chalk not far from Hambledon Hill to wind southeast through a green and shallow gorge until the valley opens out at Blandford. The other main streams of the chalk country rise in it – the Piddle and the Frome are both Dorset's own rivers and flow side by side into Poole Harbour east of Wareham.

Once out of the hills the river valleys are lush and fertile near the courses of the streams, where the soil is alluvial. The country beyond the flood plains, however, is less benign, forming a wedge of poor, infertile land (in geological terms Bagshot Beds) pushed into Dorset from the New Forest. This is Thomas Hardy's Egdon Heath, which he described as 'a vast tract of unenclosed wild', but which the twentieth century has largely tamed. Tanks from the Army camp at Bovington tear up its centre, the Forestry Commission pinion it with plantations of dark conifers in the west, and Bournemouth and Poole have obliterated it in the east. Yet on the southern side of Poole Harbour, between Wareham and Shell Bay, lies a scarcely accessible corner of the old Egdon

Heath, where you may still feel the grandeur and awesomeness of which Hardy wrote at the opening of *The Return of the Native*.

Poole Harbour brings us to the coast, by common consent Dorset's most splendid feature – though it can hardly be called one feature when its variety encompasses so many. From the gentle harbour at Christchurch, overlooked by the great Priory, to the final westerly flourish at Lyme Regis, the coast presents such changes of mood and style as may be rarely seen elsewhere in so short a distance. Christchurch Harbour itself, into which the Dorset Stour and Hampshire Avon flow in a common estuary, gives way beyond the preserved wilderness of Hengistbury Head to the settled and sea-walled front of Bournemouth and the Branksome Park and Canford Cliffs areas of Poole. Here yellow sandstone cliffs of no great height are crowned if not by houses and hotels then by pines and gorse, and penetrated by narrow valleys, or chines, which served as routes for smugglers. The northern shore of Poole Harbour, together with the Sandbanks peninsula, is similarly burdened by the hand of man, but to its south and west, indented by innumerable creeks and inlets, and bejewelled by green islands ranging from the giant Brownsea to tiny islets, the Harbour, than which none is finer save that of Sydney, remains almost immaculately without human settlement.

Past the sand dunes of Studland come the first chalk cliffs, the headland of Handfast Point, where the Old Harry Rocks in sacrificial white await destruction by the sea. Beyond the chalk cliffs lies Swanage, grey and Victorian, and south of that a strip of tough oolitic limestone, broken off by the sea at Peveril Point and stretching like a protective wall as far as Worbarrow Bay. Between the oolite and the chalk lies a green valley of wealden clay, studded with villages built of the grey stone named after Purbeck itself and quarried out of the coastal hills.

From Worbarrow, where the grey is briefly succeeded by cliffs of autumnal colouring, the chalk again takes over, and stretches almost as far as Weymouth. Not, however, without interruption. At Lulworth Cove a remnant of the Purbeck coastal hills, which once extended much further west than they do now, protects the chalk just behind it from the

8

sea's battering, but has been pierced. Through the breach the sea has pounded away that great circular lagoon so well known to tourists and exploited by those who exploit them. Round the corner, at Stair Hole – where the fantastically contorted rock strata testify to the power of the forces that shaped our landscape – the formation of another lagoon has begun. From here to the end of the chalk cliffs is what many people feel to be the most attractive section of the Dorset coast – brilliant white cliffs topped with rolling downland turf, all utterly lonely and remote, inaccessible except on foot. Not far from Lulworth, Durdle Door continues to defy the elements and probability, a huge natural folly, a triumphal arch leading nowhere and celebrating nothing.

The central part of the coast makes a dull contrast except where Weymouth enlivens it. And, of course, one must not forget (indeed one cannot for it dominates the seascape for many miles) the Isle of Portland, which on the map looks like a great pendant slung below the coastline, and from the mainland like the head of a monstrous bird resting on the sea. Portland has a curiously bare landscape, pitted with quarries whence its hard, grey stone has been taken for St Paul's Cathedral, Waterloo Bridge, and many other important structures in London and elsewhere.

Westward from Portland a coastal plain beneath more chalk downs is protected by that curious formation, the Chesil Bank, an 18-mile-long spit of pebbles running as far as Bridport, and separated from the mainland between Portland and Abbotsbury by a narrow inlet called the Fleet. The pebbles grow in size from west to east, being fine and almost granular near Bridport, and inches across in the east, the progression being so marked that local smugglers were said to have been able to tell the whereabouts of their landfall from the size of the stones beneath their feet.

Between Abbotsbury and the Devon border at Lyme Regis the coastline is as grand as that of Purbeck. The rocks that form the coastal hills of west Dorset are older than those of the east – in fact there is a continuous exposure from Lyme eastward of rocks of the Jurassic type, from Blue Lias to Forest Marble, a matter of importance and delight to all geologists. The nomenclature of these rocks testifies indeed to the work of scientists along this seaboard, for they called several of them after their Dorset provenances – Black Ven Marls, named from the great cliff near Lyme, Eype Clay, from the hamlet near Bridport, Down Cliff Sands and Clay, and Thorncombe Sands from two of the great trio of cliffs not far off, as well as Bridport Sands. Variegated and undulating, the coast presents a tapestry of gold and grey and blue. From the cliff tops, such as Thorncombe Beacon and Golden Cap (the highest point on the whole south coast of England) there are panoramic views out to sea and inland into Devon and Somerset. Below, the rocks are extraordinarily rich in fossils of ammonites and belemnites. Not far from Lyme was found the first complete fossil of an ichthyosaurus ever unearthed.

Indeed, behind its coast West Dorset is full of unexpected scenic gems. The geology is confused and unsystematic, and the scenery reflects the confusion – rounded hills of grotesque shapes, twisted and winding valleys with steep sides, and small towns and villages wedged between. In the far west, north of Lyme, is a round, clay-floored bowl, the Vale of Marshwood, which contains hardly a village, but bears an interlacing of narrow lanes like those of Devon.

If there is no scenery typical of Dorset, so also its towns and villages display equal variety. Apart from the Christchurch-Bournemouth-Poole conurbation Dorset has no really large centres of population, but that single one is quite sizeable, and because of its reputation with tourists and holidaymakers its fame is wider spread than that of any other part of Dorset. Weymouth comes far behind in size (though not necessarily in attractiveness) and otherwise only Dorchester, the county town, associated closely and appropriately with Dorset's greatest literary figures, Hardy and Barnes, has any pretensions. Wimborne Minster, Sherborne, Shaftesbury, Lyme Regis, Bridport, Swanage, Blandford Forum – how the names roll off the tongue! – are small and essentially country towns, living largely (one excepts the seaside resorts, of course) on the commerce that derives from the rural industries in their own neighbourhoods.

In Bournemouth and Poole the twentieth century has savaged both the primeval heathland and the townscapes of the past. Bournemouth it is true, still has some of its Victorian heritage, not all of it (*pace* Sir John Betjeman) worth keeping, but Poole has quite recently destroyed so much of its eighteenth-century core that what remains, carefully preserved though much of it now is, stands only as a hint of what ought to have survived. Both towns, where they are not just Kingston Bypass suburban, are now largely dominated by the clumsy, angular carcasses that characterise post-war European architecture.

Yet in Blandford and Bridport Dorset has essentially eighteenth-century towns of irresistible charm. The blend in Weymouth of eighteenth- and nineteenth-century Georgian with the prettiest Victorian outweighs even the mediocrity of the more recent residential spread. Much of Lyme Regis still looks as it must have done to Jane Austen, when she wrote so affectionately of it in *Persuasion*. In Sherborne, largely built of warm, honey-coloured Ham stone, Dorset possesses a rare gem, a sparkling blend of the architecture of six centuries, crowned by a splendid Abbey.

The county's smaller settlements, the villages and hamlets, are again considerably varied in their architecture. Where good local building stone was available it was used. So, in the Isles of Purbeck and Portland the houses are of the famous grey stone quarried from the fossil-rich limestone beds of which the land is formed. In West Dorset from Abbotsbury to west of Bridport the buildings are pale gold because the local oolite of this colour was easily to be had and good to build with. In the northwest the villages round Sherborne have much Ham stone from Somerset. Cob with thatch survives in quantity in many Dorset villages, especially in the centre of the county – the best known is Milton Abbas. The black and white half-timbering that lends charm to the Midlands you do not find in Dorset, but timber-framed houses are to be seen, for instance in Cerne Abbas as well as elsewhere, though usually in isolation. The characteristic building material of the chalk area is flint, not often used in unbroken masses, but in combination with ashlar or brick. Many churches in the centre and east of the county have alternating horizontal bands of flint and ashlar, or these materials are worked in a chequer pattern, as at Wimborne St Giles. Older houses may echo this fashion, which is later modified by the substitution of brick for dressed stone.

In general Dorset's architecture lacks the spectacular. There is no cathedral to compare with Winchester or Salisbury, Exeter or Wells. The finest church in the county is the Priory at Christchurch – a recent acquisition from Hampshire – which, though it is no cathedral, would certainly stand out in any English county for its sheer beauty. Wimborne Minster, Milton Abbey, and Sherborne are the only other large churches, and they too, comparatively modest though they are in scale, have their own attractions – Sherborne its fan vaulting and its grandeur, Milton its setting in a Capability Brown landscape, and Wimborne its architectural variety and warmth of detail.

The smaller churches have suffered too much from nineteenth-century meddling, but many are still interesting enough. The satisfying little Norman church at Studland, for instance – the most complete of its period in the county – doubly reinforces the pleasure of a visit to the village and its sandy beach. Winterborne Tomson, in isolation with just a farmhouse nearby, is also Norman, and even smaller, but it has all its eighteenth-century fittings and was restored with money derived at his own wish from some of Thomas Hardy's effects. Chalbury also has its eighteenth-century furnishings, including a fine three-decker pulpit. Puddletown no-one should miss. Its monuments, its furnishings, its airy Perpendicular plan, and its Thomas Hardy associations (his father played the violin in its gallery) all make it an essential call. The church at Whitchurch Canonicorum, in the far west, has its own unique claim to attention, for in addition to the graciousness of its architecture it boasts alone among the churches of England the shrine of its own patron saint, a Saxon lady called St Wita. Other good churches may be seen at Blandford, Bere Regis (more Hardy associations, this time with *Tess of the D'Urbervilles*), Sydling St Nicholas, Affpuddle, Cerne Abbas, Wimborne St Giles, Lyme Regis, and Abbotsbury – and this rather arbitrary list omits, for instance, St Peter's, Dorchester, Fordington, Cranborne, and St George's Reforne (on Portland), to name only a few.

Apart from its churches Dorset can show a wealth of country houses of real interest. The grandest is Forde Abbey, which incorporates much of the former monastic complex from which it takes its name, and dates back to the twelfth century. Athelhampton; St Giles' House, the home of the Earls of Shaftesbury; Sherborne Castle, the core of which was built for Queen Elizabeth's favourite, Sir Walter Raleigh; Kingston Lacy; Melbury House; and Mapperton are all showpieces. Their owners open to the public occasionally quite a number of other houses, many dating back to Tudor times or earlier, and well justifying a visit.

For many people today Dorset is the South Wessex of the writings of Thomas Hardy, and indeed much survives which Hardy wrote about or is associated with him. So many of his poems and short stories, as well as the longer works, are set in the Dorset countryside, and so many of his characters, especially those often richly comic rural folk who provide a dramatic antiphony to the central action in the novels and in parts of *The Dynasts*, are part of his Dorset setting, that the sheer vitality of his writing has imposed on us all to some degree preconceptions which may distort our vision of what the county is and how it looks. But other reactions are legitimate. Where Hardy saw menace and gloom it is possible sometimes to find tranquillity. What moved him to pessimistic reflection may have more cheerful associations for some. He wrote as a poet and a teller of tales whose drama he used Dorset's undoubted mysteriousness to heighten. Great artist though he was, it can do no harm to counterbalance his influence with that of Dorset's second literary figure, William Barnes, born forty years before Hardy and less accessible because he wrote in dialect. The effort to read him is worth making, though, for in all the troubles of his life he seems to have retained a sunny optimism that fits Dorset just as well as Hardy's view. He, too, thought of Dorset when he wrote

The zwellen' downs, wi' chalky tracks
A-climmen' up their zunny backs,
Do hide green meäds an' zedgy brooks,
An' clumps o' trees wi' glossy rooks,

An' hearty vo'k to laugh and zing,
An' parish churches in a string,
Wi' tow'rs o' merry bells to ring,
An' white roads up athirt the hills.

This contrast between the philosophies of two great writers emphasises the variety to be found in the county. To appreciate why so many people, once acquainted with Dorset, become lifelong enthusiasts about it, and agonise over every threat to its character, whether from the oil industry or the tourist trade or the industrialisation of agriculture or the suburbanising minds of bureaucrats – in short, from the unthinking philistinism of too many people with short-term vested interests – reading about it and looking at pictures is not enough. You must go and see for yourself.

The Plates

CERNE ABBAS

A village of great visual attractiveness, Cerne Abbas has some of Dorset's most interesting associations. The chalk downs above it are not only studded with barrows and 'Celtic' fields, but bear that very singular figure, the Cerne Abbas Giant, which is now in the care of the National Trust. This huge idol cut in the turf of Giant's Hill – he is 180 feet long – probably dates back to pre-Roman times and a native fertility cult. In the old churchyard (by the Abbey ruins) a clear spring flows, which legend says was produced by none other than St Augustine to facilitate the baptism of the local heathen. He had need of miracles – for the cult of the Giant was alive for centuries after.

In the Middle Ages the Abbey from which the village gets half its name was of some importance, but now only fragments remain, including an elaborate gateway like that at Forde. The parish church, a handsome and spacious building with a stone Madonna over the west window of the tower, contains an unusual stone screen of the fifteenth and wall paintings of the fourteenth century. Across Abbey Street (the second house from the left in our photograph) is 'Barnwells', the house in which in 1594 a commission sat to investigate charges of atheism against Sir Walter Raleigh.

The buildings of the village, many of them Georgian or earlier, fit together with remarkable harmony, and for many people Cerne Abbas is the favourite among all Dorset's settlements.

CHALK DOWNS NEAR OSMINGTON

The Dorset Downs bear two figures cut in their turf. One is the Cerne Abbas Giant, a cult figure of respectable antiquity. The other is King George III, whom in 1815 the citizens of Weymouth had depicted on the south-facing slope at Osmington riding resolutely eastwards on horseback. This was intended as a token of their gratitude and loyalty to a monarch whose patronage of their town had brought them much prosperity as a fashionable seaside resort.

The setting of the turf figure is quite typical of Dorset downland – bare hilltop overlooking intensively farmed lowland. At one time these hills were largely used for grazing sheep, but today much of the flinty soil has been ploughed up, a fate which has fortunately not overtaken the hill in our picture.

At Osmington itself John Constable spent his honeymoon, and left a number of sketches, not only of the village but also of Bowleaze Cove and Weymouth Bay. Osmington is a bright little place with a church, heavily restored in 1846 but containing an anonymous monument with three inscriptions that are curious on several counts. The third, cut vertically on the edge of a tablet, reads, 'Here is not the man who in his life with every man had law and strife'. Connoisseurs may enjoy trying to interpret that!

THE CHESIL BANK AND ABBOTSBURY SWANNERY

Abbotsbury, at the head of the Fleet, where the Chesil Bank joins the mainland, has a swannery which dates back at least to 1393 and is sometimes open to the public. On the hill above, clearly visible in our illustration, is St Catherine's Chapel, a weathered little building of golden stone, immensely sturdy, and furnished with a stone tunnel-vaulted roof like nothing else in the south of England.

The village of Abbotsbury itself, its main street with its raised pavement made up almost entirely of cottages built in that same local stone, was long associated with the medieval abbey, of which remnants are still to be seen. The most striking is the great tithe barn, dating from about 1400 and about 90 yards long, of which half is still roofed and in use. One can also see a stone gatehouse and some other fragments, while stones from the abbey have been used for some of the village houses. The church has a west gallery, a Jacobean pulpit with bullet-holes from the Civil War, and in the chancel a delicate, plastered barrel roof dating from 1638.

The views from the hills round about are spectacularly good. St Catherine's and Abbotsbury Castle (an Iron Age hill fort to the west) offer superb prospects of the sea coast in both directions, and for a look into remote distances inland as well one may go to a point above Portesham, some miles off. Here stands an absurd tower called Hardy's Monument erected in 1844 to the memory of Sir Thomas Hardy, Nelson's Flag Captain and a man of Dorset. From here you can see half the county.

BRIDPORT – TOWN HALL AND MAIN STREET

Best visited out of season, because of the traffic that jams the main streets in summer, Bridport dominates the history and geography of west Dorset. The main roads converge on it, the economic demands of its rope-making industry gave rise for centuries to the cultivation of hemp in its hinterland (though the plant now grows only wild) and even today it is the most populous town near the coast west of Weymouth.

Rope-making, incidentally, is the origin of Bridport's most obvious feature, its extremely wide streets, across which yarn, twine, and ropes spun and twisted in long gardens behind the houses were hung up to dry. The industry, which dates back to the Middle Ages here, still flourishes, though nowadays its raw materials are artificial fibres.

The Town Hall is the most conspicuous building because of its height, achieved by the addition of the clock tower and cupola about twenty years after its original construction in 1785–6. The town centre indeed has a wealth of other eighteenth-century buildings, with some older ones worth looking at, especially the so-called 'Chantry' in South Street. Its origin and purpose are unknown, and its date is guessed to be four-teenth or fifteenth century.

THOMAS HARDY'S BIRTHPLACE, HIGHER BOCKHAMPTON

The brick and thatch cottage in which Thomas Hardy was born is now in the care of the National Trust and open to the public. As everyone knows, Hardy was essentially a man of Dorset, rooted in the county, educated in it. His parents' parish church was at Stinsford, which figures as 'Mellstock' in *Under the Greenwood Tree*, and his heart was buried in the churchyard there. He went to school in Dorchester, at Hardy's School (founded by, and named after, an Elizabethan Thomas Hardy, who was a common ancestor of the novelist and of Nelson's Flag Captain) and was apprenticed to John Hicks, a Dorchester architect. In 1884 he settled at Max Gate, near Dorchester, and lived there until his death 44 years later.

It is not too much to say that the country and people of his ancestral county were the most important of all single influences on his writing, which was as highly coloured by Dorset as he has coloured our view of it. Dorchester and Michael Henchard, Bere Regis and Tess Durbeyfield, Egdon Heath and Diggory Venn, Maiden Castle and Sergeant Troy – every reader of Hardy can make dozens of similar connections. The birthplace in a still quiet and remote hamlet and half surrounded by woodland, seems utterly appropriate.

OLD HARRY ROCKS

These gleaming splinters of chalk at the southern end of Studland Bay reach towards their more famous counterparts, the Needles. Indeed, at one time a ridge of chalk stretched across from Dorset to the Isle of Wight until the sea breached it. Now, Handfast Point, off which Old Harry stands, is the easternmost end of the chalk downs that form the spine of the Isle of Purbeck, and an exhilarating place it is, too. You have to walk there – up from Studland to the north or Swanage to the south, or along Nine Barrow Down and Ballard Down from Corfe Castle to the west – and the country to landward is superb. It was hereabouts that E. M. Forster had in mind when he wrote in *Howard's End* that the best way to show a foreigner England would be to stand him on the final section of the Purbeck Hills, east of Corfe: 'Then system after system of our island would roll together under his feet'. And indeed, from the tops of these downs one may look over Poole Harbour and the flat lands beyond to the hills of central Dorset, then Cranborne Chase, and the edges of Salisbury Plain. 'Seen from the west', wrote Forster, 'the Wight is beautiful beyond all laws of beauty'. Bournemouth and Poole on the left (bigger, more obtrusive, uglier, than before the First World War, when Forster wrote) represent habitation and commerce – and a little imagination will still take us, as it took him, at least as far as London!

MILTON ABBAS

The village today is an artificial creation, a piece of village planning which arose from the ruthlessness of an eighteenth-century magnate, one Joseph Damer, Lord Milton and Earl of Dorchester, whom Horace Walpole described as 'moderately sensible, immoderately proud, self-sufficient, and whimsical'. The village when he came centred on the Abbey church and the great house which had been bought by a Dorset landowner on the Dissolution of the Monasteries. But for Damer's taste the village was too close to his property. He therefore proceeded to have it removed lock, stock, and barrel, using various dirty tricks to force out reluctant inhabitants, and replaced it with the work of art illustrated opposite, situated where it did not interfere with the view from the house.

The grounds of his mansion, now suitably uninhabited, he had landscaped by Capability Brown, and the house itself remodelled by Sir William Chambers. He had the grace to leave the Abbey Church standing. That it lacks a nave we cannot blame on Lord Milton, for an earlier church was struck by lightning in 1309. Of its replacement only the chancel and transepts were ever built, though in a grand style that demands a visit.

Indeed, apart from its historical interest, Milton Abbas should be visited for its aesthetic qualities. Not only are its buildings attractive in themselves, but they are set in the heart of some of Dorset's most pleasant scenery.

PORTLAND BILL

The Isle of Portland is a bleak, unattractive, but far from uninteresting block of grey oolite thrust by Nature into the Channel and left to weather. It is practically treeless – probably its only trees are those near its oldest building, the ruined Rufus Castle at Church Ope Cove – its shores are inhospitable, its villages austere.

It is most famous for its building stone, which was first used on any scale by Inigo Jones in the early seventeenth century and is now represented in many public and private buildings all over Britain, from St Paul's Cathedral downwards. As a result the island's surface is pitted with quarry workings, some of which can be seen in the photograph.

The Bill is Portland's southern tip, and must once have had some grandeur, but a large car park, and miscellaneous mean buildings as well as the nibblings of the quarrymen have put paid to that. The lighthouse is absolutely necessary for the story of Portland is full of shipwrecks. Three miles out to sea lies the notorious Shambles sandbank, which has also claimed large numbers of victims. Among them was the *Abergavenny*, commanded by the brother of the poet Wordsworth, which sank in 1805 with the loss of 300 lives.

CHESIL BANK FROM PORTLAND

The highest point of Portland is over 400 feet above sea level, overlooking the little town of Fortuneswell at the northern end of the Island. Northwest from here the Chesil Bank curves gracefully away towards Abbotsbury and Bridport. In the far background are the downs over which the Dorchester-Bridport road runs, and in the middle distance Weymouth, with Portland Harbour before it.

The road to Portland from Weymouth hugs the northern side of the Chesil Bank on a causeway, then climbs sharply within a mile to the point near which this photograph was taken. It is the only route to Portland from the mainland, and one can easily see why down the ages the people of the island were a race of their own, enjoying little contact with the outside world, and living by their own laws and (sometimes singular) customs. Because of this same inaccessibility a fortress was built at Verne at the island's top, and a convict prison, now a Borstal, not far away at Grove.

The savagery of the dour island's scenery and of the inhospitable coast was reflected in bygone centuries in the inhabitants' behaviour to shipwrecked sailors, who, both on Portland and on the Chesil Bank, were not succoured but plundered.

WEYMOUTH

Weymouth is the product of the fusion of two towns – Weymouth proper on the south side of the harbour and Melcombe Regis on the north. No one remembers Melcombe Regis any more, although it was not only the place where the Black Death entered England in 1348, but also contains everything that the holidaymaker associates with Weymouth – which seems pretty rough justice. The Esplanade and main beach, the railway and bus stations, and the main shopping centre, cinemas, and concert hall – none of them is in the original Weymouth.

Not that this really matters. The union took place before most of the town was built, and its present character is that of a lesser Brighton (which is by no means meant to be a disrespectful description). Those fine Georgian terraces on the sea front and the bow-fronted houses by the harbour, speak of the frequent visits of George III and his family, while the cheerful Victorian building has done no harm whatever. Indeed the jolly little Victorian clock tower is a real embellishment, which is more than can be said of the execrable monument to George III's Golden Jubilee.

West of the Harbour, Sandsfoot Castle, a blockhouse built by Henry VIII, crumbles into the sea, though across the bay, at Chesilton on Portland, a similar fort in excellent condition is open to the public and looked after by the Ministry of the Environment.

BOURNEMOUTH

In view of its present size and population one is surprised to find that the first building in Bournemouth was erected only in 1810. Until then its nameless site was a waste of heath and gorse that extended from Poole to Christchurch, a place of transit both for legitimate travellers and for smugglers, who hastened along its tracks or crept clandestinely up its chines.

Thanks to the boom in seaside holidays during the nineteenth century, which the mildness of its climate enabled it to exploit with special success, it became one of the most favoured and famous of all the English coastal resorts. The pines planted in its centre and by some of the chines, the gardens along the banks of the little Bourne stream that reach two miles from the front through the town's centre to the suburbs beyond, and the careful restraint which has protected the coast itself from indiscriminate vulgarisation, have given Bournemouth its special character.

Several miles of sea wall protect its yellow cliffs, below which are beaches of sand to the west and pebbles to the east. Some of its Victorian buildings have great character, and some, such as the Russell Cotes Museum, are period pieces. It is a good shopping centre, it has theatres, cinemas, and concert halls. It has also, bless it, a crowning glory which makes it incomparable among British resorts – a symphony orchestra of international standard.

SWANAGE BAY

The sandy beach and the sheltered bay are the assets which attract the holidaymaker to Swanage, which today is still a rather Victorian seaside resort. Since the town lies at the eastern end of the Purbeck wealden valley, on either side the bay is stopped by a hill. On the north lies the huge gleaming edge of Ballard Cliff, the end of the Purbeck chalk ridge. To the south the oolite mass of Peveril Point reaches into the sea, its strata twisted, with sharp reefs below the surface – perhaps those on which a Viking fleet was destroyed by a storm in 877.

Beyond Peveril Point, to the south-west, is Durlston Head with the Tilly Whim caves, which lead below it to a broad rock platform formed by quarrying. Similar platforms occur in several places along the coast, for instance at Dancing Ledge and Winspit. Indeed, for centuries quarrying gave the whole area some importance, and the predominant grey of the buildings at its centre marks Swanage as a Purbeck town built of Purbeck stone. Until the late nineteenth century the stone was trans-shipped here from quays called bankers, where it was manhandled into boats which took it to freighters lying offshore. The coming of the railway in 1887 saw the end of this activity and the demolition of the bankers, which have left no trace on the holiday scene.

SWANAGE – THE MILL POND

This much-photographed spot is undoubtedly the most picturesque part of Swanage, so long as you look at it from the right viewpoint. Move round, and the sight is more ordinary.

The sad truth is that Swanage has few architectural charms, though it can show several curiosities to be appreciated by people with a sense of humour. For instance, a memorial to King Alfred's victory over the Danes in 877 is crowned by cannon balls. The clock tower, which was removed in 1863 from London Bridge, where it was a memorial to the Duke of Wellington, lacks a clock. The Town Hall has a façade by Wren, originally on the Mercers' Hall in Cheapside. And on Durlston Head is a huge terrestrial globe in local stone, while the walls of Durlston Castle are peppered with geographical information and a gloomy prophecy from *The Tempest*.

If, however, one tires of the quirky, a consolation is that the three major country houses of the Isle of Purbeck, in their lordly green settings, are none of them far from Swanage. These are Encombe (once the home of Pitt's reactionary Lord Chancellor, Lord Eldon), Smedmore, the most homely of the three, and Creech Grange, where peacocks walk the gardens.

WAREHAM

Long before the rise of Poole, Wareham was the main settlement on the shore of Poole Harbour, a port of significance, the point of entry to the Frome valley from the sea, and dominating the road into Purbeck by Corfe. The Saxons threw up earthworks all round it in the form of a square, and one may still walk them on three sides of the town. The Danes none the less sacked it, and it suffered the same fate at the hands of King Stephen.

Today it is frankly (discounting the summer traffic) a backwater. The estuary of the Frome and the shore of the Harbour, through centuries of silting up, have left it a mile inland, and it has not been used as a port for over six centuries. But even now the best approach to it is by boat from Poole, across the Harbour and up the river. Wareham is still largely an eighteenth-century town, and because of a devastating fire in 1762 not much survives from earlier days. The little church of St Martin, however, has much Saxon fabric and some medieval wall paintings, as well as a fine effigy by Eric Kennington of Lawrence of Arabia, who lived and was killed in a motorcycle accident not many miles away.

The heath on the southern shore of the Harbour towards Arne and Studland has some of its primeval eeriness even today. Between Wareham and Corfe are claypits, one of which, the Blue Pool (disused and flooded, of course!) attracts coach-loads of tourists because of the pure blue colour of the water in sunshine.

POOLE – THE CUSTOM HOUSE

Poole today, contiguous as it is with Bournemouth, spreads over a great tract of what was once heathland. Canford Cliffs and Branksome Park, much of them still Victorian and Edwardian, meander amid trees and lawns on the east. Suburbia of a less attractive kind oozes northward. Yachts based on moorings at Parkstone and Sandbanks enliven the surface of the Harbour, and at Sandbanks, on the seaward side of the peninsula, is some of the best bathing in the area.

At the old centre of Poole quite sizeable ships still load and unload freight on the Quay, and fine pottery is manufactured nearby. Amid the bustle you may look across the Harbour to the great tree-clad block of Brownsea Island, now the property of the National Trust, and beyond it to the bare hills of Purbeck. The custom house stands on the site of an earlier one which saw a famous raid in 1747 by a large gang of smugglers, whose cargo of tea had been intercepted, and lay there. Opposite is the early nineteenth-century Harbour Office building, from whose colonnade this photograph was taken, and nearby is the fifteenth-century Town Cellars and its contemporary, the Old Town House, or Scaplen's Court, which is a fine relic, now used as a museum.

Round the parish church and to its north, especially in Market Street, with the little red brick Guildhall and its excellent staircase, efforts have been made to preserve the remains of the eighteenth century. Indeed, here it is that one senses the essence of the town despite all the later accretions.

ATHELHAMPTON

Near Puddletown, on the main road from Dorchester to Poole, Athelhampton House stands behind a screen of trees in its elegant garden, which also contains a sixteenth-century dovecote. From the south, half the front is fifteenth century and half sixteenth, the older part being battlemented and furnished with an oriel window which reaches from the ground almost to the eaves.

This window looks out from the great hall, of which the impressive and unusual timber roof remains unaltered, with its extraordinary cusped arch-braces. It has also a minstrels' gallery and good linenfold panelling. This part of the house was built by Sir William Martyn, who was Lord Mayor of London in 1493 and whose descendants lived here for a century and are buried in the so-called Athelhampton chantry in the parish church at Puddletown.

Athelhampton is one of several country houses of great architectural and historical interest whose owners often played important parts in the county's history. Kingston Lacy, near Wimborne Minster, for example, was the later home of the Bankes family, so intimately concerned in the last days of Corfe Castle. St Giles' House, at Wimborne St Giles, belongs to the Earls of Shaftesbury, the first of whom was one of the Parliamentary leaders in the Civil War, and played a rather different part after the Restoration. Other houses like Athelhampton itself, and Forde Abbey (the most splendid of them all) have changed hands often by purchase, but the aesthetic appeal of their fabric compensates for any loss of historical or sentimental interest.

MAIDEN CASTLE

Out of the plain south of Dorchester rises a solitary hill crowned by an enormous hill fort, the largest in Dorset and one of the largest in Britain, whose triple ramparts, 60 feet high, measure over two miles in circumference. This colossal work has a history – or rather a past, for it is prehistoric – that goes back to Neolithic times, but what is visible today dates from the late Iron Age, when it contained a permanent fortified settlement with metalled streets.

It was stormed and taken in AD 43 by a Roman legion under the command of an officer who later became the Emperor Vespasian, and the County Museum in Dorchester has many relics of the fight, including the skeleton of a young man with an arrowhead still lodged in his spine. After the Roman conquest most of the inhabitants were probably settled in what is now Dorchester, but later a pagan temple whose foundations can be seen was built at the eastern end.

Near Dorchester are two other prehistoric earthworks. Maumbury Rings, just by the Weymouth road south of the town centre was a Neolithic henge monument, which the Romans adapted for use as an amphitheatre. Much later it was used for public executions – the last witch to be burned alive in England was executed here, and in the eighteenth century it was the site of a gallows. The other earthwork, Poundbury, is a sizeable fort, but stands no comparison with Maiden Castle.

CHRISTCHURCH

The most easterly town in the county, and until 1974 a part of Hampshire, Christchurch is distinguished for two main features. The first is
the natural harbour, nowhere near as large or beautiful as that of Poole,
but useful to yachtsmen, and overlooked on the southwest by the
enigmatic mass of Hengistbury Head, where men settled as long ago
as the Bronze Age. The other feature is the great Priory church, which
vies with Sherborne Abbey as Dorset's most important and impressive
example of ecclesiastical architecture. It incorporates work of every
century from the eleventh to the sixtcenth, much of it of great beauty.
The nave and transepts are Norman, while the east and west ends,
including the ambulatory and sanctuary are later, and no one should miss
the excellent misericords of thirteenth- to sixteenth-century date in the
choir. The reredos (about 1350) is an overwhelming sculptural creation,
which can be compared to nothing else in Dorset.

Apart from the Priory, Christchurch has the remains of a twelfth-
century castle by the river north of the church. It was presumably built
for Richard de Redvers, to whom Henry I gave the town. Apart from a
handful of Georgian buildings, which give it just a little character,
Christchurch has little else to show. For most of us it is identified with
the Priory – which is perhaps enough to endow it with a great deal of
distinction.

SHAFTESBURY

A Saxon hilltop town accessible only up steep rises, and looking over the great escarpment of the Dorset downs, Shaftesbury has a past which, in combination with its site, promises much. Its Benedictine nunnery, founded in 888, was enormously wealthy, and the town once had 12 churches and a castle. Unfortunately, not much of this past glory remains. The ground plan of the abbey is visible, the foundations having been excavated. A lead casket is to be seen which contains the bones of a young man, quite probably the actual remains of King Edward the Martyr brought here from Wareham four years after his murder. Only one of the medieval churches still stands, and not much of that is original. There is nothing of the castle.

One comes to Shaftesbury, then, not for its relics of the past, but for its setting. From Park Hill, by the site of the abbey, one has an exhilarating view over the Vale of Blackmore towards Bulbarrow Hill, and from the top of Gold Hill (as the illustration shows) one of the most romantic sights in England. The cobbled street dips sharply below Park Hill, along the foot of a great retaining wall between whose huge buttresses, now green with lichen, sheep were penned during the Martinmas Fair in November. The simple cottages form an extraordinary foil to the massive masonry, while beyond is the lush countryside of Blackmore Vale.

LYME REGIS

Crammed into and flowing up the sides of the valley of the little river Lym, Lyme Regis perches at the very western end of the Dorset coast in a bowl formed by the coastal hills in which the river has cut a gap. The attractive church stands on the edge of a cliff, and the whole town is built on slopes, except, of course, along the shore itself. Everywhere in the centre are eighteenth- and nineteenth-century buildings that create an atmosphere of their period.

The famous Cobb, the quay and breakwater which protects Lyme's artificial harbour, the source of its prosperity at least until the end of the seventeenth century, is still used. But today only small boats shelter there, and as a port Lyme has no commercial importance. Readers of Jane Austen will be glad to know that the steps down which Louisa Musgrave fell in *Persuasion* are still to be seen leading from the lower to the upper Cobb.

The coast in either direction is magnificent. The cliffs over the Devon border are grey and crumbling, those eastwards, towards Charmouth, also unstable, especially after heavy rain, but more variegated, grey shading into bluish black, or as at Black Ven capped with a layer of gold. Small streams like the Lym have cut through them, and at their mouths are little villages – Charmouth, Chideock, and Eype – all dwarfed by the tumultuous country round them.

ABBOTSBURY – THE TITHE BARN

The Abbey at Abbotsbury was a Benedictine foundation built by one Orc, a member of King Canute's bodyguard. By the Dissolution it was a community of middling wealth (ranking behind Shaftesbury, Sherborne, Milton, and Cerne, for instance) but it has left us its magnificent tithe barn, which is one of the largest in England, and certainly unique in Dorset.

Indeed, of the Dorset abbeys not much is now left to see. Only the ground plan of the church at Shaftesbury, the richest of all, is still visible. At Bindon, near Wool, some forlorn ruins and the fishponds remain. Cerne can show a splendid gatehouse and, again, some fragments, Tarrant (at Tarrant Crawford) only a church with some fourteenth-century paintings. Milton, with its great church and its buildings transmogrified into a country house, which is now a school, and Sherborne, whose buildings were partly incorporated into an existing school, fared better. Best of all is Forde, where the remains of the abbey have become a country house of real distinction, set in a carefully landscaped park.

The Abbotsbury barn stands in a rough working setting, presumably much as when it was built, and its sheer size gives us some idea of the economic importance of even a medium-sized monastery.

WIMBORNE MINSTER

The Minster church dominates the little town which bears its name, and which originally grew up beside it. It is a curious building, partly because it is constructed of stone in grey and several shades of brown, partly because of the outlandish battlements and pinnacles which surmount its crossing tower. This arrangement replaced a spire which collapsed in 1600. Inside, the fine Norman piers of the crossing, the chevron-ornamented nave arcade, and the three-light Early English east window are the main features to note in an interior with many attractive smaller details. An astronomical clock said to be the work of a Glastonbury monk in 1320 still works in the west tower, and outside, high up in the same tower, a little red-coated Grenadier parades every quarter of an hour.

   The town centre has in many places (particularly in the street called West Borough) a distinctly eighteenth-century feel, while the Priest's House – now a museum – can show interior features dating from the later Middle Ages. The site of the Minster itself has yielded Roman remains, including a bit of tessellated paving still in place under glass. Within easy driving distance you can go still further back in time to the Iron Age at Badbury Rings, and to Bronze Age and Neolithic times with the Dorset Cursus and the great group of barrows on Oakley Down near Cranborne.

SHERBORNE ABBEY

In 998 a Benedictine Abbey was founded in Sherborne, though little of the original Saxon building remains, except a fragment at the west end of the Abbey church. What we see today, a warm, golden building, is essentially Norman, the magnificent fan vaulting of the nave, like the cladding of the piers, disguising the early date of this lovely church's core. Some of the Abbey buildings are incoporated in the school, which adjoins the church.

The fifteenth-century almshouses, to the south-west of the church, should be seen for their original stained glass, and for a superb near-contemporary triptych, probably German, behind the altar in the chapel. Elsewhere, Sherborne can offer buildings of every century from the sixteenth onward. Just outside the town are two castles – the older one medieval and ruined ('slighted' in the Civil War, like Corfe, by its Parliamentary captors), and the later one that Sir Walter Raleigh built as a gentleman's residence. This was added to by later owners, and one of them had Capability Brown landscape the park. We see it now as he intended – an embellishment worthy of the town whose name it carries.

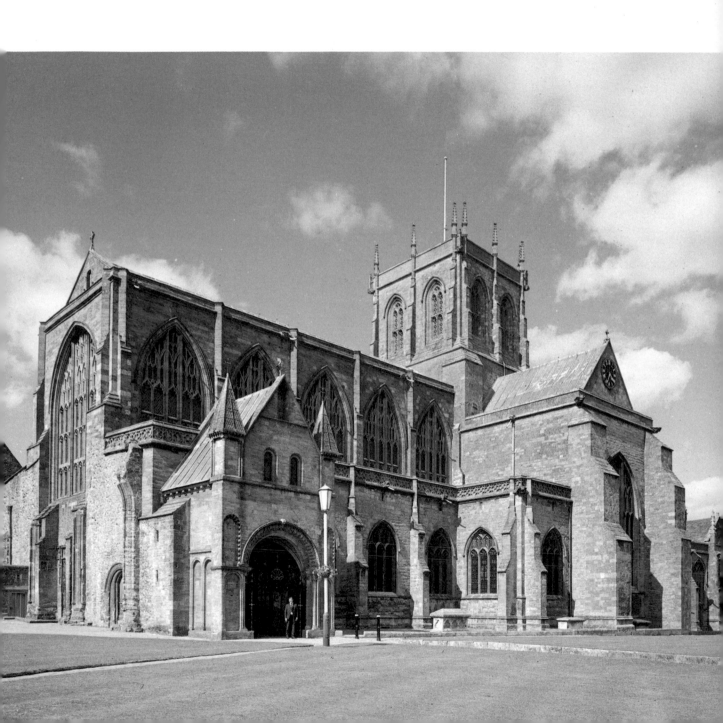